The Window Seat

A higher plane of spiritual understanding.

Angela Attiah

KINGDOM ALLY
United in Power & Purpose

Most **KINGDOM ALLY** products are available for special quantity discounts for bulk purchase relating to sales promotions, premiums, fundraising, and educational needs.

THE WINDOW SEAT by Angela Attiah
Published by Kingdom Ally
5250 Grand Avenue, Suite 14-320
Gurnee, Illinois 60031
www.kingdomally.com
info@kingdomally.com

This book, or parts thereof, may not be reproduced in any form, stored in a retrieval system, or transmitted in any form by any means—electronic, mechanical, photocopy, recording, or otherwise—without prior written permission of the publisher, except as provide by United States of America copyright law.

Book cover design by Angela Attiah.

Copyright © 2020 by Angela Attiah
All rights reserved.
Visit the author's website at www.angelaattiah.com

Scripture quotations marked AMP are taken from the Amplified® Bible (AMP), Copyright © 2015 by The Lockman Foundation. Used by permission. www.Lockman.org

Scripture quotations marked ESV are taken from the ESV® Bible (The Holy Bible, English Standard Version®), copyright © 2001 by Crossway, a publishing ministry of Good News Publishers. Used by permission. All rights reserved.

The Window Seat

Scripture quotations marked MSG are taken from THE MESSAGE, copyright © 1993, 2002, 2018 by Eugene H. Peterson. Used by permission of NavPress. All rights reserved. Represented by Tyndale House Publishers, a Division of Tyndale House Ministries.

Scripture quotations marked NKJV are taken from the New King James Version. Copyright © 1982 by Thomas Nelson, Inc. Used by permission. All rights reserved.

Scripture quotations marked NIV are taken from the Holy Bible, New International Version®. Copyright © 1973, 1978, 1984 by International Bible Society®. Used by permission. All right reserved worldwide.

Scripture quotations marked NLT are taken from the Holy Bible, New Living Translation, copyright © 1996, 2004, 2007, 2013, 2015 by Tyndale House Foundation. Used by permission of Tyndale House Publishers, Inc., Carol Stream, Illinois 60188. All rights reserved.

Scripture quotations marked TPT are from The Passion Translation®. Copyright © 2017 by BroadStreet Publishing® Group, LLC. Used by permission. Al rights reserved. thePassionTranslation.com.

ISBN: 978-1-7352527-0-4

Printed in the United States of America.

Dedication

To all who hear voices in their head and talk to themselves—you're not crazy after all! You've actually been gifted by God to traverse through the higher realms.

Now go forth in your divine calling, under the tutelage of Holy Spirit, and wield this gift for the glory of God!

Table of Contents

Introduction 2
Chapter 1: One With the Mind of Christ 6
   Doubt's Debut 7
   Personal Lesson Plans 19
   Co-Creators with Christ 23
Chapter 2: God Is In the Details 26
   Playtime Prayers 27
   Locksmith on Location 30
Chapter 3: Partnering With Word & Spirit 38
   Discerning Danger 41
   Pineapple & Potatoes 45
Chapter 4: Hone My Hearing 54
   Navigated Prayers 55
   Subway Shield 60
Chapter 5: Power of Words & Agreement 66
   Bondage or Blessings 67
   Talking Truth 71
Chapter 6: Enduring Trials & Testing 78
   Gorilla Gift 79
   Being Scourged 84
   Sonic Blast 87
Chapter 7: Pitfalls of Pride 94
   Deliverance for Dollars 96
   Praying for Profit 101
   Televangelist Trap 111

Introduction

This book is intended for the Holy Saints who desire to go higher into the heavenly realms, as Jesus opens the door to greater understanding.[1]

Soon after receiving a powerful infilling of the Holy Spirit, I was overcome by a voracious hunger to serve the Lord. At that time, and in my limited understanding, I believed the only way to properly do so was to attend seminary school and become a pastor.

The Lord, in His great kindness, spoke to me one day, while I was eagerly researching seminaries, and said, "You are to be taught by My Spirit,[2] not by man." Therefore, it is by His grace alone that I offer you this book of divine

---

[1] Revelation 4:1
[2] 1 John 2:27

lessons learned along the way.

The purpose of this writing is to share God's wisdom and revelation, in order to bring freedom from destructive mindsets, which hold believers captive and hinders their spiritual growth. It is the knowledge of the truth that sets us free,[3] and many of God's people are being destroyed due to lack of knowledge.[4]

In this season of life (Fall 2019), I will soon begin my sixth year of discipleship under the tutelage of the Holy Spirit, and yet in some ways, it feels like my journey has only just begun. Following Jesus these past five years has come at a great cost to me personally, yet my love for Him grows deeper every day.

The testimonies shared throughout this book are a sampling of divine insights which have molded and strengthen my faith in Jesus. Remember, we overcome Satan by the blood of the Lamb and the word of our testimonies![5]

---

[3] John 8:32
[4] Hosea 4:6
[5] Revelation 12:11

As you glean upon my experiences — both good and bad — I pray the eyes of your heart are enlightened with wisdom and revelation, so you may know the perfect will of God for your own life.[6]

May it be the Lord's thoughts and desires you engage with as you read through these pages, for just one word from Him changes everything!

Grace and peace to you all, as friends and family in the faith!

---

[6] Ephesians 1:18

Chapter 1: One With the Mind of Christ

Oh how amazing it is to know the Creator of the Universe wants to personally speak with each one of us! Who could ever imagine an ordinary human could fellowship with the grandest mind of them all!

No longer do we have to drudge through life aimlessly and without purpose. What a privilege we are given through our partnership with God, as He reveals the good and perfect plans He's laid out for us, including divine foresight of the dangerous traps that lie ahead.

By embracing the mind and likeness of Christ, we may fulfill our purpose on the Earth.

So how do we *actually* embrace the mind of Christ, you ask? Here's a story to help illustrate how I came to understand this radical concept.

Doubt's Debut

One day I was excitedly sharing, with a small group of people from church, some of the impactful conversations I was experiencing with the Lord.

A gal in the group pointedly asked me, "So what does His voice actually *sound* like?"

"Well," I said, with a slight hesitation, "kind of like my own thoughts, I guess, but somehow different."

The woman then pressed in further with a hint of sarcasm in her voice, "So *how* can you tell the difference between *His* voice and *your* own thoughts? I mean, *how do you know you're not just making it all up in your head?*"

"Um, honestly, I don't quite know," I said, stammering in my response.

And with that, I left quickly, totally deflated by the question. Suddenly, my mind was clouded by overwhelming doubt!

I kept playing the same question over and over in my head, "How *do* I know the difference between Your thoughts and my thoughts, Lord?" For weeks, this question plagued me until I could hardly concentrate on anything else. It was absolutely maddening!

I had inquired of other believers, scoured the internet, searched through the Bible, but mostly I found myself crying out to God because I so longed for Him to tell me directly. I wanted to hear *His* voice in my heart again.

Suffice it to say, I started questioning myself further. *"I did heard Him before, right? Why can I not hear Him now? Certainly that was not just made up in my head!"*

Then one day I am literally down on my knees begging the Lord to tell me, when to my surprise, He abruptly breaks into my thoughts with:

God: "Daughter!"

Me: "Yes, Lord?"

God: "Have I not given you the mind of Christ?"

Me: "Um, yes, Lord."

God: "Am I in you and you in Me?"

Me: "Yes."

God: "Then stop trying to separate us! We are one and the devil is trying to convince you we are not. Know that the greater your desire grows for Me, the more My thoughts become your thoughts."

Me: "Oh wow, that is *so* cool! Thanks, Lord! I love you!"

God: "I love you too, sweetheart."

Like a little child pulling on my Abba Daddy's pant leg, I was pleading for *His* voice to comfort me. Though it seemed He may have been a bit annoyed with the begging nature of my cry, He knew just how to capture my attention and put my mind at ease.

Oh what comfort filled my heart to know His

thoughts were becoming my thoughts!!

Even now, as I enter my sixth year as a disciple of Jesus, it is still my greatest desire to please Him—not because I'm afraid of His punishment, per se, but because I desire to show Him my love.

Consider the impact of God's promises for His disciples, offered through His Word (emphasis added):

John 17:20-26 NLT

20 "I am praying not only for these disciples but also for all who will ever believe in me through their message. 21 <u>I pray that they will all be one, just as you and I are one—as you are in me, Father, and I am in you. And may they be in us so that the world will believe you sent me</u>.

22 "I have given them the glory you gave me, so <u>they may be one as we are one</u>. 23 <u>I am in them and you are in me</u>. May they experience *such perfect unity that the world will know that you sent me and that you love them as much as you love me.* **24** *Father, I want these whom you have given me to be with me where I am. Then they can see all the glory you gave me because you loved me even before the world began!*

25 *"O righteous Father, the world doesn't know you, but I do; and these disciples know you sent me.* **26** *I have revealed you to them, and I will continue to do so.* <u>*Then your love for me will be in them, and I will be in them.*</u>*"*

John 6:56-57 NLT

56 *"<u>Anyone who eats my flesh and drinks my blood remains in me, and I in him</u>.* **57** *I live because of the living Father who sent me; in the same way, anyone who feeds on me will live because of me.*

1 Corinthians 2:16 NKJV

16 "For, 'who has known the mind of the Lord so as to instruct him?' But <u>we have the mind of Christ</u>."

John 14:15-31 NIV

15 "<u>If you love me, keep my commands</u>. 16 And I will ask the Father, and he will give you another advocate to help you and be with you forever— 17 the Spirit of truth. The world cannot accept him, because it neither sees him nor knows him. <u>But you know him, for he lives with you and will be in you</u>. 18 I will not leave you as orphans; I will come to you.

19 "Before long, the world will not see me anymore, but you will see me. Because I live, you also will live. 20 On that day you will realize that <u>I am in my Father, and you are in me, and I am in you</u>.

21 "<u>Whoever has my commands and keeps them is the one who loves me</u>. The one who loves me will be loved by my Father, and I too will love them and show myself to them.

22 "Then Judas (not Judas Iscariot) said, 'But, Lord, why do you intend to show yourself to us and not to the world?'

23 "Jesus replied, '<u>Anyone who loves me will obey my teaching</u>. My Father will love them, and we will come to them and make our home with them.

24 "Anyone who does not love me will not obey my teaching. These words you hear are not my own; they belong to the Father who sent me. 25 All this I have spoken while still with you.

26 "But the Advocate, the Holy Spirit, whom the Father will send in my name, will teach you all things and will remind you of

everything I have said to you.

27 *"Peace I leave with you; my peace I give you. I do not give to you as the world gives. Do not let your hearts be troubled and do not be afraid.*

28 *"You heard me say, 'I am going away and I am coming back to you.' If you loved me, you would be glad that I am going to the Father, for the Father is greater than I. 29 I have told you now before it happens, so that when it does happen you will believe. 30 I will not say much more to you, for the prince of this world is coming. He has no hold over me, 31 but he comes so that the world may learn that <u>I love the Father and do exactly what my Father has commanded me</u>. Come now; let us leave."*

It was the voice of doubt creeping in through that woman's questions, which caused an invisible barrier to rise up between the Lord and

I—just as Satan caused Eve to doubt God in the garden.[7]

The Word reveals the Lord has made His home within us, as the temple for His Holy Spirit.[8] So ask yourself this question, "Would Jesus model being led by the Father's voice, if He did not offer us the same capability?"[9] Of course not!

Take some time to really meditate on John 10 and the powerful revelation that you *can* hear His voice (emphasis added).

John 10:1-18 MSG

1-5 "Let me set this before you as plainly as I can. If a person climbs over or through the fence of a sheep pen instead of going through the gate, you know he's up to no good—a sheep rustler! The shepherd walks right up to the gate. <u>The gatekeeper opens the gate to</u>

---

[7] Genesis 3:1
[8] 1 Corinthians 6:19
[9] John 5:19-30; John 8:28; John 12:49-50; John 14:10

him and the sheep recognize his voice. He calls his own sheep by name and leads them out. When he gets them all out, he leads them and they follow because they are familiar with his voice. They won't follow a stranger's voice but will scatter because they aren't used to the sound of it.

6-10 "Jesus told this simple story, but they had no idea what he was talking about. So he tried again. 'I'll be explicit, then. I am the Gate for the sheep. All those others are up to no good—sheep stealers, every one of them. But the sheep didn't listen to them. I am the Gate. Anyone who goes through me will be cared for—will freely go in and out, and find pasture. A thief is only there to steal and kill and destroy. I came so they can have real and eternal life, more and better life than they ever dreamed of.

11-13 "I am the Good Shepherd. The Good Shepherd puts the sheep before himself, sacrifices himself if necessary. A hired man is not a real shepherd. The sheep mean nothing to him. He sees a wolf come and runs for it, leaving the sheep to be ravaged and scattered by the wolf. He's only in it for the money. The sheep don't matter to him.

14-18 "<u>I am the Good Shepherd. I know my own sheep and my own sheep know me</u>. In the same way, the Father knows me and I know the Father. I put the sheep before myself, sacrificing myself if necessary. You need to know that I have other sheep in addition to those in this pen. I need to gather and bring them, too. <u>They'll also recognize my voice</u>. Then it will be one flock, one Shepherd. This is why the Father loves me: because I freely lay down my life. And so I am free to take it up again. No one takes it from me. I lay it down of my own free will. I have the right to lay it down; I also have the right to take it up again. I received this authority personally from my Father."

As the testimony of doubt revealed, Satan and his evil cohorts can influence the thoughts and actions of anyone who is not completely yielded to the leading of Holy Spirit, *even if they are believers.*

The following passage about Jesus rebuking Peter offers some additional insight into this claim (emphasis added).

Matthew 16:21-23 TPT

---

21 *"From then on Jesus began to clearly reveal to his disciples that he was destined to go to Jerusalem and suffer injustice from the elders, leading priests, and religious scholars. He also explained that he would be killed and three days later be raised to life again.*

22 *"Peter took him aside to correct him privately. He reprimanded Jesus over and over, saying to him, "God forbid, Master! Spare yourself. You must never let this happen to you!*

> **23** "*Jesus turned to Peter and said, 'Get out of my way, you Satan![c] You are an offense to me, because your thoughts are only filled with man's viewpoints and not with the ways of God.'*"
>
> **Footnote:**
> c. Or "*adversary.*" *Jesus is equating Peter's display of character to that of Satan. Peter was not possessed by Satan, but speaking from Satan's realm and speaking demonic wisdom.*

Thank God we have been given the mind of Christ to help us navigate the thoughts and ways which are higher than man's![10]

Personal Lesson Plans

When God reveals a specific truth of Scripture to me, He instructs me to transform those verses into personal declarations, in order to come into

---

[10] Isaiah 55:8; 1 Corinthians 2:16

alignment with His personalized plan for me in that season.

The Word says we are given every spiritual blessing in the heavenly realms through Jesus Christ,[11] though it seems there is a plan and appointed time to appropriate each blessing to the believer, based on their position of influence or maturity level.

As with any inheritance, the release is often linked to the recipient reaching a particular age of maturity, or satisfying certain conditions.

We serve a very personal God who is the Author and Perfecter of our faith.[12] He knows exactly what level of learning each person is capable of receiving, in any given moment.

Our part is to simply trust He's mapped out a personalized course for our lives, then come into alignment with the lesson plan of each day and season.

One day, upon entering a restaurant, the Lord

---

[11] Ephesians 1:3
[12] Hebrews 12:2

invited me to practice using the prophetic gift to relay His message to the server.

I asked Him for a word of knowledge, and He showed me a ladder leaning against a house, between two windows. I was given the understanding the server was doing some home remodeling.

Then suddenly my breasts began to tingle, as if I was preparing to nurse a child, and I saw a quick vision of a kiddie pool.

When I asked the Lord what the tingling and vision meant, He said, "This is a new believer, and only capable of ingesting spiritual milk at this time, so keep it simple."

When the server approached the table, I said, "I'm practicing hearing the voice of God and believe He has a word of encouragement for you. May I share it with you?"

She cautiously said, "Sure," as if she was bracing herself for what was to come. When I asked if she was doing some exterior work on her house, she said, "Yes! I'm actually having my windows replaced!"

The Lord then spoke through me and said her mother was going to be ok. Tears began to stream down her face as she confirmed her mother had been ill. We then prayed together for the Lord to heal her.

I am amazed at how receptive people are to hearing what God has to say — even if only to be entertained! But when His word touches a person's heart, it then has the ability to spark a deeper curiosity within them.

She then said, "Where do *you* go to church? I've never met a Christian like you!" As the Lord instructed me, I shared with her about the gifts of the Holy Spirit and how they are available to believers today. I then directed her to some online resources to help get her started.

People are so hungry for that supernatural connection with our loving God!! Please know that I don't share any of this to boast in myself, because it all points back to JESUS! He's the One who has made it all possible!

As you spend time with the Lord and step out in faith, remember the simple words of Jesus spoken to Thomas, "Stop doubting and *just believe*."[13]

Isn't it just as easy to *believe* you can hear His voice, as it is to doubt? You get to choose what you believe, so get in line with the Word of God! I've encountered prolonged periods of doubt myself, so know I am also walking this truth out every single day.

When I catch myself under doubt's influence, Holy Spirit reminds me, "Though the righteous fall seven times, they shall rise again,"[14] so don't beat yourself up—just start again with a fresh perspective!

Co-Creators with Christ

After some time of building intimacy with the Lord, He began to change the way I viewed serving Him. Instead of asking what I could do *for* the Lord each morning, I was encouraged to

---

[13] John 20:27
[14] Proverbs 24:16

ask, "What are *we* going to do today, Lord?"

It's a small change in perspective, but hugely impactful in the way we go about our day, together *with* Him instead of merely doing *for* Him.

This type of mentality brings us from the position of servanthood into one of friendship with God.[15]

I have discovered that God is looking for partnership, not robots who merely carry out His commands. He could have easily created us that way, but instead chose to gift us with the free will to choose.

Truth be known, there are many times I wish He would just issue a daily task list to me, but that completely removes the intimate element of connecting with Him personally.

Healthy relationships require ongoing interaction and communication with one another, and it's no different with the Lord.

---

[15] John 15:15

Further Meditation

1. Have you ever allowed doubt to cloud your faith or belief in hearing God's voice?

2. What Bible passage speaks to your heart in this season?

Chapter 2: God Is In the Details

It's so freeing to fully comprehend that we serve a God who cares for every detail of our lives, down to knowing the exact number of hairs on our head![16] Did you know He actually *delights* in directing our steps?[17] The Bible says so!

Anyone who studies science and nature — from to the microscopic to mammoth levels — will likely agree that there is a grand design in it all. It is God Almighty who is the great Artist and Architect of creation, paying close attention to every detail.

---

[16] Luke 12:7; Matthew 6: 25-33; 10:30; Psalm 56:8; 139:13-14
[17] Psalm 37:23

I encourage you to take a moment and read or listen to Job 38-41. In these powerful chapters, God takes Job on a virtual tour of just a few of the details taken into account with creation. It's mind-boggling!

Playtime Prayers

One summer day, a few friends and I gathered together to pray over one of the gals taking a trip back to India. Her young son was not in school that day, so we elected to meet at the local park, hoping it would provide an outlet of fun for him, and a little freedom for her to receive prayer.

Upon arriving at the park, we realized there were no other children around, leaving this little guy clamoring to his mom for entertainment.

In that moment, I casually lifted up a prayer saying, "Lord, we'd really like to spend some time praying for our sister. Would you please send a playmate for her son?"

Less than 15-20 seconds later, this vibrant little girl came out of nowhere, prancing up the sidewalk and calling out, "Who wants to play? Who wants to play?"

We all looked at each other with stunned expressions, then began praising the Lord for answering our prayer.

I said, "Wow! The Lord really does care about the smallest prayers." Immediately, I heard Him say, "That's not a small prayer to Me!"

It was important to the Lord for us to gather in prayer, *and* for her little boy to have fun. He knew just what we needed before we even asked![18]

Our friend's son and that little girl played so well together while we prayed — with our eyes open, of course!

As we gathered around the picnic table, I shared a testimony about the time I asked the Lord to help me find a hairstylist. At that time in my life, I had racked up some pretty awful salon experiences, so I was just a tad bit apprehensive to try anyone new.

---
[18] Matthew 6:8

Those of you reading, who've had bad salon experiences, can relate to what I'm saying!

My first year as a disciple, I was participating in the Alpha class — a course on exploring Christianity. There was a session about the power of prayer and how God cares about *every* aspect of our lives.

One evening after class, I went home and decided to test out this concept by asking God to help me find a hairstylist.

The next day, a new friend called and was unusually cheerful in her greeting. When I asked why, she proceeded to tell me about this great new hairstylist she found through church.

I bubbled up with excitement as I shared the prayer request from the night before, and eagerly asked for the stylist's contact info.

Was that mere coincidence? No way! I never mentioned a word about the request to my friend, nor did she know I was looking for a hairstylist! Oh and it turned out to be a fantastic experience!

Locksmith on Location

On another occasion, I locked my keys in a moving truck. Sounds dangerous, right? Haha, well the truck wasn't actually moving—it was a Uhaul truck.

While driving this Uhaul truck, my other key ring had fallen out of my bag and onto the floorboard. I made a mental note to grab them once I got to the destination point, but with all the excitement of driving that big 'ole truck, I just plain forgot about the keys falling!

It was the end of a very long day, and a friend was following behind me to give me a ride back from the truck lot. It was after-hours and the rental office was closed, so I locked the doors and deposited the truck key into the designated drop box before getting into my friend's car.

About half way back to my new place, it finally dawned on me I had not grabbed the keys from the floor. *Arrgg!!*

I quickly asked my friend to turn around and take me back to the rental place. Curiously she asked, "What can you do? The office is closed and the key is in the drop box!"

"I don't know," I said, "but the Lord will help somehow."

To our surprise, when we arrived back to the truck location, there was a man waiting in the parking lot.

While we were pulling up to the door, he got out of his truck and waved to us, asking, "Did you order a locksmith?"

"No, but we sure need one!" I exclaimed.

He said someone called for one, but no one ever showed up. Then he smiled and said, "Well I guess this one's on the house!"

My friend and I just stared at each other in amazement as he used a tool to quickly unlock the truck door and retrieve my keys.

Friends, I could share many many other testimonies of how the Lord has surprised me with answers to, what seemed like, insignificant prayers. On so many occasions He has helped, which is why I depend on Him for everything!

Truly there is nothing too small in the eyes of our Abba Father, and He really does delight in helping us! Do not let the devil lie to you, saying God is too busy or doesn't care about your needs. The Lord is all knowing and ever present to help us!

Don't just take my word for it, friends. Ask Him yourself. Many times we don't have because we don't ask, or are asking with the wrong motives.[19]

Ask with sincerity, knowing He's a good good Father who desires to care for His children in healthy, loving, and protective ways.

Take a look at what His Word has to say about this (emphasis mine):

Philippians 4:6 NKJV

6 "<u>Be anxious for nothing</u>, but in everything by prayer and supplication, with

---

[19] James 4:2-3

thanksgiving, <u>let your requests be made known to God;</u>"

Psalm 121:1-2 ESV

1 "I lift up my eyes to the hills. From where does my help come? 2 <u>My help comes from the Lord</u>, who made heaven and earth."

Psalm 46:1 TPT

1 "God, you're such a safe and powerful place to find refuge! <u>You're a proven help in time of trouble—more than enough and always available whenever I need you.</u>"

Romans 8:28 TPT

28 "So we are convinced that <u>every detail of our lives is continually woven together to fit into God's perfect plan of bringing good into *our lives, for we are his lovers who have been called to fulfill his designed purpose."*

John 14:14 TPT

14 "Ask me <u>anything</u> in my name, and I will do it for you!"

Proverbs 3:5-6 TPT

5 "Trust in the Lord completely, and do not rely on your own opinions. <u>With all your heart rely on him to guide you, and he will lead you in every decision you make</u>. 6 "<u>Become intimate with him in whatever you do, and he will lead you wherever you go</u>."

Psalm 37:5 NLT

5 "Commit everything you do to the LORD.

Trust him, and <u>he will help you</u>."

Philippians 4:19 TPT

19 "I am convinced that my <u>God will fully satisfy every need you have</u>, for I have seen the abundant riches of glory revealed to me through the Anointed One, Jesus Christ!"

Hebrews 4:16 AMP

16 "Therefore let us [with privilege] approach the throne of grace [that is, the throne of God's gracious favor] with confidence and without fear, so that we may receive mercy [for our failures] and <u>find [His amazing] grace to help in time of need [an appropriate blessing, coming just at the right moment]</u>."

Further Meditation

1. When have you experienced miraculous or just-in-time help?

2. Are you "serving for" or "serving with" God?

Chapter 3: Partnering With Word & Spirit

Jesus said the Father longs to have sincere worshipers who worship and adore Him in Spirit and in Truth.[20]

It is imperative for believers to learn how to embrace both the written and spoken words of God. As the testimonies you've been reading about in this book demonstrate, God desires to interact with us in our every day lives!

We cannot operate solely on the written Word, nor is it safe to engage only with the Spirit. Both are meant to work in tandem to provide a balanced understanding of God's expectations,

---

[20] John 4:24

character, and will for any given situation.

Jesus is the Word and the Truth.[21] The Holy Spirit always points us to Jesus and leads us into all Truth.[22] One does not work without the other.

And let us not forget the Father!

Jesus made the way for us to be reconciled with the Father of all, who designed the plans for each person's life.[23] Then we receive the Holy Spirit, who is sent to reveal the depths of the Father's heart, and to empower us, like Jesus, to carry out His plans.[24]

It's important to know, God is not confined only to His written Word. Meaning, He is at liberty do and say things that go beyond what is written in His Word, though it is to serve as the benchmark for God's character. Just as the Beloved John shared—all the wonderful works of Jesus cannot be contained in the Bible.[25]

---

[21] John 1:1-3, 1:14, 14:6, 17:17
[22] John 14:26, 16:3
[23] Jeremiah 29:11; Proverbs 16:9, 19:21
[24] 1 Corinthians 2:10; Ephesians 2:10
[25] John 21:25

We need the Holy Spirit to enlighten the written Word of God for us. Otherwise, we are merely acquiring heading knowledge of Scripture, without ever fully understanding its application to our lives.

Consider what Jesus said to the religious leaders who relied only on the written Word of Scripture to guide them (emphasis added):

John 5:37-40 NLT

37 "And the Father who sent me has testified about me himself. <u>You have never heard his voice or seen him face to face,</u> 38 and you do not have his message in your hearts, because you do not believe me—the one he sent to you.

39 "<u>You search the Scriptures because you think they give you eternal life. But the Scriptures point to me!</u> 40 Yet you refuse to come to me to receive this life."

Discerning Danger

A friend and I were traveling out of town late one evening and decided to pull over for some refreshments. As soon as we exited the highway, I felt a strange eeriness in the atmosphere and sensed danger.

My first instinct was to get right back on the highway and stop further up the road, but in the naïveté of being a fairly new disciple of Christ, I resolved to press through the fear, pridefully rationalizing, "We are children of God, so no harm will come to us. Besides, light always overcomes the darkness!"[26]

After entering the store and perusing the aisle for snack food, the strange feeling of danger intensified. Guarded in our approach, I quickly took the items up to the register and noticed a young twenty-something man standing next to the counter.

I motioned to my friend with a nodding glance to make sure she saw the guy too. It

---

[26] 1 John 5:18; Psalm 91:10; John 1:5

appeared he was coming off the influence of some kind of drug. He had that jonesing look in his eyes and was trembling with the shakes from, what I guessed to be, withdrawal symptoms.

"Oh no!" I thought, *"What have I gotten us into here. This guy could be planning to rob the place. Please keep us safe, Jesus!"*

I kept the guy fixed in my peripheral vision as I made small talk with the clerk and my friend. With debit card in hand, I let out a loud gasp and nearly jumped out of my skin when the total rang up to $6.66![27]

Immediately I heard the Lord say, "That feeling you are experiencing is the gift of discernment.[28] You must heed My warning and leave right now!"

I shot a wide eyed look to my friend and said, "We gotta get out of here *now*!"

That was such a valuable lesson learned in the importance of weighing out those internal

---

[27] Revelation 13:18
[28] 1 Corinthians 12:10; Hebrews 5:14

warning signals with the Lord. I realized afterwards that I hadn't even consulted the Lord before charging ahead, instead merely relying upon my head knowledge of Scripture.

We need both the Word and Spirit of God to guide us. Again, it's the Holy Spirit who illuminates the application of the Word and what Jesus would do in any given situation.

I'm just so grateful no harm came to us that night. The Lord reminded me that He often sends signals to redirect our path away from danger.

Joseph was warned, through a dream, to flee with Jesus and Mary to another city when King Herod was after them.[29] Paul and Silas were forbidden by the Spirit to preach in Asia.[30] Even Jesus withdrew from the pharisees who were plotting to kill Him.[31]

Like the testimonies revealed in the last

---

[29] Matthew 2:13-23
[30] Acts 16:6
[31] Matthew 12:14-15

chapter, we are invited to seek His direction in *all* things, big or small.

Check out the following passages relating to discernment (emphasis added):

1 Corinthians 12:8-11 TPT

8 "For example: The Spirit gives to one the gift of the word of wisdom. To another, the same Spirit gives the gift of the word of revelation knowledge.

9 "And to another, the same Spirit gives the gift of faith. And to another, the same Spirit gives gifts of healing.

10 "And to another the power to work miracles. And to another the gift of prophecy. <u>And to another the gift to discern what the Spirit is speaking</u>. And to another the gift of speaking different kinds of tongues. And to another the gift of interpretation of tongues.

11 "Remember, it is the same Holy Spirit who distributes, activates, and operates these different gifts as he chooses for each believer."

Hebrews 5:13-14 ESV

13 "for everyone who lives on milk is unskilled in the word of righteousness, since he is a child. 14 <u>But solid food is for the mature, for those who have their powers of discernment trained by constant practice to distinguish good from evil</u>."

Pineapple & Potatoes

One afternoon, my daughter, who was four at the time, came down with a fever and began complaining about stomach pains. I had been faithfully walking with Jesus for about two years at that point, and had witnessed many supernatural healing miracles first hand, including the regeneration of my own thyroid!

As I had done so many times before, within those two years, I began praying against the illness, commanding it to come out and the fever to leave my daughter, in Jesus' name.

After some time of praying, with no visible signs of change, I suddenly felt a tap on my shoulder. Turning around, I sensed the presence of the Lord in the room and looked over to see a vision of Him leaning against the door frame with His arms folded across His chest.

He then said, "Would you like to ask *Me* what to do?"

Oh my! In that moment, I felt the holy fear of God come over me—not like I thought He might punish me, or anything like that. I had simply realized the majesty of His name.

Here I was using the name of Jesus, and I hadn't even sought His counsel! Again, I was merely relying on my knowledge of Scripture.

As I humbly bowed my head in reverence to

His holiness, I responded with, "Oh yes, Lord. Please tell me. What should I do?"

He kindly instructed me, "Let the fever run its course and check back with Me in the morning."

I was bewildered by the simplicity of His instructions, but did as He directed.

Throughout the night, I received revelation and understanding about the natural way our bodies are designed to fight infection with fevers.

Friends, so many times we are quick to administer meds, when we may actually be interfering with the body's natural defenses. The Lord is the ultimate Healer, and as such, we must submit to His chosen remedy, whether received through medical practices, or natural remedies.[32] He should be the One to direct our steps.

The next morning, I awoke to my daughter drenched with sweat, crying in pain as she held her little stomach. With a quick check, I realized the fever had actually increased.

---

[32] Ezekiel 47:12; Revelation 22:2

In a panic, I desperately cried out, "Lord, I know you love her more than I do and don't want her to suffer. What should I do???"

What He said next really caught me off guard and caused me to question if I was really hearing Him.

The Lord matter-of-factly said, "Give her fresh pineapple followed by potatoes."

Puzzled, I asked, "What? You want me to give her pineapples and potatoes?" The Lord confirmed, "Yes. Now go quickly."

The whole time I am getting us dressed to go to the store, I am being bombarded with thoughts of how insane I am, telling me,*"You should be ashamed to think God would heal through pineapples and potatoes, of all things!,"* and, *"How unspiritual you are for not having the faith to heal her supernaturally!"*

By the time we arrived at the store, I knew the demonic voices were not going to stop until I put my foot down and said something.

So, in a quietly stern voice, I whispered aloud, "I'm doing as the Lord instructed me, so back off demons!"

Now these are the moments when one might appear crazy to an unknowing bystander, but that's what it took for the dark thoughts to stop!

When we got back home, I immediately gave my daughter the fresh cut pineapple, which she ate quickly. While boiling the potatoes, the Lord instructed me to wait about a half hour before giving them to her. He added, "Keep them plain and season only with a little olive oil."

I did exactly as He instructed, and within an hour after giving her the pineapple, my daughter really needed to go to the bathroom.

Wanting to be a comfort to her, I held her little hands while she released the most horrendous smelling substance you could ever imagine. Oh my, it was foul!

Soon after she was done on the toilet, she literally started skipping around the house and singing. She was absolutely fine and completely back to normal in no time.

Over the next several days, the Lord began teaching me how important it is to come to Him for guidance in *all* things. Not only do we waste time when we pray in our own strength and knowledge, but we may be treading outside the will of God with our prayers. Gratefully His grace covers us while we are still learning.

Take some time to consider and meditate upon these passages (emphasis mine):

Acts 19:13-17 NIV

---

13 "Some Jews who went around driving out evil spirits tried to invoke the name of the Lord Jesus over those who were demon-possessed. They would say, "In the name of the Jesus whom Paul preaches, I command you to come out." 14 Seven sons of Sceva, a Jewish chief priest, were doing this. 15 One day the evil spirit answered them, "Jesus I know, and Paul I know about, but who are you?" 16 Then the man who had the evil spirit jumped on them and overpowered them all. He gave them such a beating that they ran out of the house naked and bleeding.

17 "When this became known to the Jews and Greeks living in Ephesus, <u>they were all seized with fear, and the name of the Lord Jesus was held in high honor</u>."

Matthew 7:21-27 TPT

21 "Not everyone who says to me, 'Lord, Lord,' will enter into the realm of heaven's kingdom. It is <u>only those who persist in doing the will of my heavenly Father</u>. 22 On the day of judgment many will say to me, 'Lord, Lord, don't you remember us? Didn't we prophesy in your name? Didn't we cast out demons and do many miracles for the sake of your name?' 23 But I will have to say to them, 'Go away from me, you lawless rebels! I've never been joined to you!'

24 "<u>Everyone who hears my teaching and applies it to his life</u> can be compared to a wise man who built his house on an unshakable foundation. 25 When the rains fell and the flood came, with fierce winds beating upon his house, it stood firm because of its strong foundation.

26 "But <u>everyone who hears my teaching and does not apply it to his life can be compared to a foolish man who built his house on sand.</u> 27 When it rained and rained and the flood came, with wind and waves beating upon his house, it collapsed and was swept away."

John 5:19-20 ESV

19 "So Jesus said to them, "Truly, truly, I say to you, <u>the Son can do nothing of his own accord, but only what he sees the Father doing</u>. For whatever the Father does, that the Son does likewise. 20 For <u>the Father loves the Son and shows him all that he himself is</u>

<u>doing</u>. And greater works than these will he show him, so that you may marvel."

John 8:28-29 TPT

28 "You will know me as 'I AM' after you have lifted me up from the earth as the Son of Man. Then you will realize that <u>I do nothing on my own initiative, but I only speak the truth that the Father has revealed to me.</u> 29 I am his messenger and he is always with me, for <u>I only do that which delights his heart.</u>"

Further Meditation

1. Have you ever been disappointed by the Word of God not fulfilling a purpose, as you believed it would?

2. Are you intentionally connecting with both the Word of God and the Holy Spirit?

Chapter 4: Hone My Hearing

One day I asked the Lord to please hone my hearing so I would be more sensitive to the Holy Spirit. The Oxford Dictionary defines *honing* as:

1. *sharpen (a blade)*

2. *refine or perfect (something) over a period of time.*

Now allow me to interject something here — I truly believe it is the Holy Spirit who prompted me to ask this question because I really couldn't come up with it on my own. Anytime a new concept is introduced, I first ask for Holy Spirit to teach me.

Again, once you've determined to set your

mind on the Lord, right away the Holy Spirit begins customizing that personal lesson plan, made just for you.

In the process of learning, be prepared and know, sometimes God may ask you to do something really bizarre, but trust He has purpose in it—and no, it's not to make you look foolish!

What He may be asking of you could be the answer to someone else's prayer. I'll share another testimony to illustrate.

Navigated Prayers

Alright, so to begin this training of honing my hearing, the Lord instructed me to get in my car.

"Ok, where to, Lord?" I asked.

"Just start driving, and I'll navigate." He said.

So turn after turn, mile after mile, I chose to believe He was instructing me. After I was in the car for about an hour, with no clear direction on where exactly we were going, I began to hear those doubting thoughts creep in saying I was delusional and making up conversations with God in my head again.

I quickly brushed them away and reaffirmed aloud, "I am God's sheep and I hear His voice, so anything opposed to that Truth needs to leave right now in Jesus' name."

Once back on track with the Lord, He directed me to a very prominent community.

Deeper into this neighborhood I drove, gazing at all the big beautiful homes with perfectly manicured lawns, just wondering where He was leading me.

Suddenly, I began to grow fearful of what He might ask me to do. Sensing my apprehension, the Holy Spirit assured me His plans are always good.

I found myself stopped in a cul-de-sac, in front of a large and stately home. I wondered who might live there and what their lives were like.

The Lord then instructed me, "Go knock on the door and offer prayer."

"You want me to just go knock on an absolute stranger's door and offer prayer? But Lord, they'll think I'm crazy!" I whined.

Thank God for His patience!

He gently assured me, saying, "Yes, sweetheart, I'm asking you to go knock on the door and offer prayer. Trust me. All will be ok."

With my heart pounding, I did as the Lord directed, but nothing could have prepared me for what happened next…

This little old man, about 80 years old, opened the door, and with a low voice he said, "Yes? May I help you?"

Nervously, I introduced myself, saying, "Hi, my name's Angela. I'm here to pray for you. I mean, *can* I pray for you? Or um, would you like prayer for anything?"

The man gazed at me strangely and asked in a bewildered tone, "You're here to pray for *me*?"

"*Yep, he definitely thinks I'm nuts!*" I thought. But determined to be obedient, I proceeded with, "Yes, sir, I am. Is there something specific I can pray about for you?"

He then invited me to come inside.

Trusting the Lord was not walking me into some mass murderer's home, I accepted his invitation, all the while thinking, "*Ok, Lord, help me know what to say. Oh, and please please please keep me safe!*"

The man then proceeded to tell me his wife had recently passed away and he was *just* asking the Lord, "Who's going to pray for me now?"

He went on to share, with tears in his eyes, how his wife had faithfully prayed for them throughout their marriage. She sounded like a devoted woman of God to me!

Even as I type this, my eyes fill with tears of gratitude that the Lord would use me to answer that man's prayer.

I was not there to replace his wife in any way,

but for the Lord to reveal Himself to the man, and prove He was attentive to his prayers also.

The presence of the Lord began to fill the room as we both entered into prayer with awe and gratitude for His tremendous kindness. He truly is near to the brokenhearted![33]

That experience forever marked me and I can remember thanking the Lord as I left, saying, "You can do that to me anytime!"

Yes, I was so very nervous at first, and especially as I stepped inside the house, but I chose simply to trust in the Lord's goodness.

What a great privilege it is to be the Lord's body in the Earth, co-laboring to carry out His good works.[34]

Immediately after leaving the man's house, I began praising the Lord, jumping in the air and giving virtual high-fives to the holy angels I envisioned around me! I felt so empowered by God's great love!

---

[33] Psalm 34:18
[34] Philippians 2:13; 1 Corinthians 3:9, 12:27; Colossians 1:8

Subway Shield

The Holy Spirit then led me across the county to another section of town that was completely opposite to the prestigious neighborhood I was leaving.

This particular town is known for its high crime rate and drive by shootings. I was quickly reminded *by the Holy Spirit*, "If the Lord is with us, who can be against us?"[35] The Lord Himself was leading me there, so again, I was able to move forward with confidence.

The Lord led me into a Subway shop and directed me with, "Order a drink, then sit down and wait for further instructions."

I did as the Lord instructed and began to wonder what He was setting me up for this time. Right in that moment, my eyes were drawn to a young man in the parking lot, walking hurriedly towards the door. I'd say he was about mid-to-late twenties, quite muscular, and outfitted in what one might describe as gang attire.

---
[35] Romans 8:31

Not wanting to judge a book by its cover, I thought to myself, *"Could he be the reason I'm here?"*

As soon as the young man put his hand on the door handle to enter the shop, he looked up at me with this wide-eyed look of pure shock.

He suddenly jumped back with such a force, he nearly fell down, while scampering back into his car. The young man pulled out of that parking lot so fast it made his tires squeal!

Stunned, I asked the Lord, "What was *that* all about?"

He said, "That young man saw the light of My presence around you and was scared away. He was coming to rob this place."

Friends, there have been many times I've been walking in the direction of a total stranger, and have been met with a look of complete horror, before they quickly turned to walk in the opposite direction. Almost always they are muttering something that I can't quite make out.

At first, I took these occurrences quite personally, wondering, *"What's wrong with me? Am I doing or wearing something offensive?"*

No friends, Holy Spirit shared, it is the light of His truth that often offends.[36]

Here are a few passages of Scripture to spur you on (emphasis added):

2 Corinthians 2:14-16 ESV

14 "But thank God! He has made us his captives and continues to lead us along in Christ's triumphal procession. Now he uses us to spread the knowledge of Christ everywhere, like a sweet perfume. 15 <u>Our lives are a Christ-like fragrance rising up to God. But this fragrance is perceived differently buy those who are being saved and by those who are perishing. 16 To those who are perishing, we are a dreadful smell of death and doom.</u> But to those who are being saved, we are a life-giving perfume."

---

[36] John 3:19

Matthew 5:11 ESV

11 "Blessed are you when others revile you and persecute you and utter all kinds of evil against you falsely on my account."

John 3:19-21 MSG

19-21 "This is the crisis we're in: God-light streamed into the world, but men and women everywhere ran for the darkness. They went for the darkness because they were not really interested in pleasing God. <u>Everyone who makes a practice of doing evil, addicted to denial and illusion, hates God-light and won't come near it, fearing a painful exposure</u>. But anyone working and living in truth and reality welcomes God-light so the work can be seen for the God-work it is."

Further Meditation

1. Have you ever been bombarded by negative thoughts that seemed contrary to your nature?

2. Ask the Holy Spirit to hone your hearing, then by faith, follow what you are hearing.

Chapter 5: Power of Words & Agreement

The Word of God declares that whatever two of us agree on in the Earth, it shall be granted.[37] And we also have the power to decree a thing, and it be established.[38] Those are very powerful statements!

So many times we are, unknowingly, walking around with thoughts and words that do not agree with God's will. This *stinkin' thinkin'* has great power to influence your steps.

If your heart is filled with negativity, pain, trauma, fear, and the like, it gets reflected in your

---

[37] Matthew 18:19
[38] Job 22:28

speech,[39] which only draws more negativity to you.

Allow me to expand on this by sharing a personal experience. I've had to unlearn a lot of *stinkin' thinkin'* myself!

Bondage or Blessings

A couple years into my journey as a disciple, I was faced with a very difficult situation. Since the Lord often reveals things to me through dreams and visions, I asked Him to show me what was going on in the spirit realm, as it related to my personal situation.

Immediately, I saw a vision of myself standing in an open field with angels and demons engaged in a battle above me.

Then I was given this understanding — depending on what I spoke, the words either empowered the angels to work on my behalf or the demons to work against me.

---

[39] Luke 6:16; Matthew 12.34

Then the Lord brought the vision down to ground level and I saw both an angel and a demon standing by waiting for me to speak.

Each time I spoke blessings and positive statements that aligned with God's Truth, the words would leave my mouth and turn into envelopes of assignments placed in the angel's hands.[40]

When I spoke negatively, about myself or anyone else, the words left my mouth and turned into chains that were then placed in the demon's hands to bind up the mind or torment the body of whomever I was speaking about, including myself.

The moment I realized I had unknowingly empowered Satan and his demons with negative words I had spoken, I quickly got down on my face and repented for speaking anything in opposition to God's truth, about myself or anyone else.

Holy Spirit brought these two verses to mind

---

[40] Psalm 103:20

as I was meditating on the visions:

Proverbs 18:21 AMP

21 "Death and life are in the power of the tongue, And those who love it and indulge it will eat its fruit and bear the consequences of their words."

James 3:10 NIV

10 "Out of the same mouth come praise and cursing. My brothers and sisters, this should not be."

Oh the power our words carry, especially as children of God! Consider how the Lord created the world—He *spoke* it into existence. And as His children, we are made in His image, meaning we share His capabilities (of course, as His Spirit allows).

Who did the Lord say He was when Moses

met him at the burning bush? The Lord said for Moses to tell the Israelites, "I AM has sent me to you."[41]

How many times do we use the phrase, "*I am…*" to explain our position about something? As children of God, our words have power!

Jesus said we who believe in Him would do the same and greater works than He did.[42] If He carried the power of words to resurrect life, as well as to curse unto death,[43] wouldn't that mean we as His followers do as well?

As I asked the Lord to help me with this, I became more aware of the implications of every word spoken, forcing me to take time and really think about the responses I offered.

Over the course of the next several days and weeks, the Holy Spirit began to show me how easily and unknowingly we actually empower demons, and limit the holy angels from working

---

[41] Exodus 3:13-14
[42] John 14:12
[43] Matthew 11:12-25

on our behalf.

I was reminded of all the times I had condemned myself by saying things like:

"How could I be so stupid?"

"I must be coming down with a cold."

"I'm always running late."

The Holy Spirit then instructed me to pray for a guard to be set over my mouth and for my lips to only speak God's truth.[44]

From that point forward, anytime a negative or defeated statement slipped out of my mouth, I would immediately repent of it, even if I was in the middle of a conversation with someone. It may have seemed strange to them, but I was determined not to give one ounce of power over to the enemy!

Talking Truth

Shortly after receiving this revelation, I had a dream which helped to solidify my

---

[44] Psalm 141:3

understanding of the Power of Words principle even further.

In the dream, I am rebuking a spirit of perversion that is coming against a loved one. With great gusto and confidence, I am commanding the evil spirit to leave in Jesus' name, but it just kept returning.

Then in the dream, I heard the Lord say, "You know, I can do so much more when you speak truth over a situation."

When I awoke from the dream, the Holy Spirit began emphasizing the importance of focusing on and speaking His truth. Sure, we are to rebuke and cast out evil spirits, but we must then replace the negative influence with God's Truth.

From that point forward, I began declaring righteousness, purity, and holiness over my loved one.

In yet another example, I was given a dream in which I was instructed to ask God to remove the phrase "I don't know" from my vocabulary, and replace it with "I am gaining understanding."

As I was waking up from that dream, a conversation I had with a sister in Christ came back to remembrance, in which she quoted the following revelation from the Lord:

"I HAVE TOLD MY PEOPLE THEY CAN HAVE WHAT THEY SAY, BUT MY PEOPLE ARE SAYING WHAT THEY HAVE."
CHARLES CAPPS, AUTHOR
THE TONGUE—A CREATIVE FORCE

As I engaged with the Holy Spirit, He led me to the book of Daniel. While reading the first chapter, suddenly this verse jumped off the page and I sensed it was to become my declaration in that season (emphasis added):

Daniel 1:17 ESV

17" As for these four youths, God gave them learning and skill in all literature and wisdom, and <u>Daniel had understanding in all visions and dreams</u>."

Throughout the day, I began declaring and thanking the Lord for this truth over my own life, because if He did it for Daniel, He would do it for me also.

After going to bed that evening, I was given a dream in which I also received the interpretation, <u>while still in the dream</u>!

God is truly magnificent and delights in giving us, His children, good things!

As was revealed in the first few chapters of this book, we must partner with the Lord in what He is doing in our personal life. He may not necessarily give you the same timing of revelation He has given me, because it will be personal to your situation and season.

Ask the Holy Spirit what He is teaching you in this season, and how to apply what you are learning to your own life. He is a very personal and attentive God!

Since receiving this revelation, I did follow the instructions to pray for "I don't know" to be removed from my vocabulary, which began an arduous training with the Lord.

I challenge you to count how many times in a day you hear or speak the phrase, *"I don't know."* I was stunned at just how infectious it was in my everyday encounters.

Now that I am aware of its affect on my spiritual walk, I am very careful to repent quickly if I slip up and say it, then I ask the Lord to grant me understanding in that particular area, as He has promised in His personal and written Word to me.

Remember, if you are a child of God, you are joined to the Anointed One who knows all things, and teaches us by His Spirit.[45] He also reveals secret mysteries to those who belong to Him.[46]

---

[45] 1 John 2:20
[46] Daniel 2:22; Psalm 25:14

Further Meditation

1. How many times in a day do you say or hear the phrase "I don't know"?

2. Ask the Holy Spirit to highlight and correct any negative language in your speech.

Chapter 6: Enduring Trials & Testing

It's important to know, there are times in life when troubles *will* come upon you, *because* of your devotion to Jesus.

Although salvation is free, it can be said that carrying the anointing of God will cost you everything. Paul Keith Davis, a servant of the Lord, once said the Lord told him, "The currency to purchase the anointing is surrendering your own will."

Ruminate a moment on the display of extravagant worship given by the woman with the alabaster box of perfume oil, which was used to anoint the feet of Jesus.[47] Many believe this jar of expensive oil would have cost the average worker a year's wages.[48]

The Bible emphatically declares we *will* suffer, and there is little you can do to fully escape this bitter truth. We must be willing to die to self.

To help me understand this personally, I was given a series of dreams and revelation at a time in which I was enduring a very difficult and lonely season of life.

This particular chapter only provides a small glimpse into the life-changing revelation I received. For a deeper exploration, check out my book, *The Victor's Crown of Life*, which offers a biblical perspective on suffering, and how it serves as a conduit for the glory of God.

Gorilla Gift

In one particular dream, I'm at a large home with my Dad and others who are like siblings to

---

[47] Luke 7:36-39
[48] Matthew 26:6-7 TPT (Footnote d)

me. As I look out the window into the back yard, I see a massive king kong gorilla! I'm confused because it has been given to us as a gift.

The scene of the dream then changes and I'm in my room getting ready for school. I spray myself with a beautiful smelling perfume, and suddenly, the king kong gorilla goes crazy to find me.

I quickly run to hide in the basement, and when I close the door, I'm disoriented by a thick layer of cobwebs and darkness. Not one sliver of light can be seen, and all I can do is cry.

The scene changes and I'm riding in the passenger seat of my Dad's truck as he's driving. Dad blows smoke all over me to disguise the smell of the perfume so the gorilla cannot find me. While he does this, I'm talking on the phone with a sibling, complaining about why it's so unfair I have to be covered with smoke and limited in where I can go because the gorilla is harassing me.

I briefly wake up from the dream and cry out

to God asking, "Why does the gorilla have to be drawn to me?"

When I fall back asleep, I'm told, **"There are times we must suffer many great hardships while in the King's service, but once our humility is proven, we will receive the same royal treatment as the King."**

How wonderful is God to give me the dream, as well as its interpretation! When we know there is purpose in our suffering, it gives us strength to press on.

In the dream, my Dad and siblings represent Father God and His children—my brothers and sisters in Christ. The perfume is symbolic for my worship of Jesus and the gorilla represents the harassment of Satan's messenger.[49]

The basement is the place of my deepest darkest fears, and the cobwebs are the plots of evil men used to ensnare me.

My Dad driving is symbolic of Father God's sovereignty over my life, and the smoke

---
[49] 2 Corinthians 12:7

represents His glory cloud which keeps me hidden from evil.

The gorilla is actually a gift, not a curse, which serves as a tool to bring me to the humble position of being completely led by God and consecrated for holy service.[50]

Some may say this theory is cruel and, therefore, not in God's character. Well, for those who are searching for purpose in their suffering, this revelation will actually be a comfort to them because it reveals God's sovereignty over every situation. He's not punishing you — He's training you to reign as a priestly king![51]

Ecclesiastes, one of the Wisdom books in the Bible, references God making both the day of prosperity and joy, as well as the day of adversity.[52] He gives and takes away life,[53] according to the workings of His master plan. Some people are used as vessels of destruction to

---

[50] 2 Timothy 2:21
[51] Revelation 5:10; Exodus 19:6
[52] Ecclesiastes 7:14
[53] Job 1:21

make the riches of His glory known to His vessels of mercy.[54]

Consider the intense trials and persecution brought against Job, King David, the Apostles, and ultimately Jesus, the Son of God.

This is a difficult message which can only be understood with the help of Holy Spirit. The carnal mind cannot comprehend the biblical purpose of suffering as a way to bring greater good.

It is my belief that this test-of-faith suffering is reserved only for those who have completely surrendered their lives to follow Jesus, no matter the cost.

There is a different kind of human suffering brought on as a result of sinful choices, whether individual, societal, or generational. I am not addressing that type of suffering in this book.

---

[54] Romans 9:22

Being Scourged

During an extended time of extreme hardship, I felt pummeled on every side of life. My family, finances, and housing were being attacked, all at the same time.

In desperation one night, I cried out to God, begging Him, "Please Lord! Tell me what I've done to deserve this punishment so I can change it!! I'm so sorry! Please please please forgive me for whatever it is. This is too much! I can't bear this anymore! Have I opened a door to the enemy somewhere? Just please tell me whatever it is I've done wrong!"

All I kept hearing the Lord say in response was, "I'm so proud of you my daughter!"

Well that just made no sense to me whatsoever, so I asked "Then why is my life in shambles?"

In that moment of questioning, I heard my phone ringing. It was my dad, Jack. The Lord had reconciled our relationship after a 34-year estrangement, which I shared in my first book,

Rescue Mission: Prisoners of Darkness.

I began to panic because my dad never called this late at night.

"Oh no!" I thought. *"Is he calling with more bad news?"* I just couldn't bare the thought of any more difficulties.

I tried to pull myself together to hide the pain I was feeling before answering the phone with a hesitant, "Hello?"

"Hey," he quickly broke in, "I don't know what you're going through right now, but I just want you to know I'm so very proud of you!"

"What did you say?" I asked with amazement. "I'm really proud of you," he said.

I could no longer contain myself and allowed the waterfall of tears to flow!

Father God had used my earthly father to convey His heart to me. He *really was* proud of me! *"But for what?"* I thought.

My dad then said, "The word of wisdom from

the Lord is not to ask *why* this is happening, but *what is the purpose for it."*

That night our bond was strengthened as I cried and shared how scared I really was due to the gravity of everything going on in my life. He listened attentively and offered such wonderful encouragement, which truly blessed us both.

I was so exhausted by the time we said goodnight and I collapsed in bed. But before I closed my eyes, I said aloud to the Lord, "Ok, I'll stop asking why this is happening. So, what is the purpose for it?"

Ever so matter-of-factly, I heard Him say, "You're being scourged."

Well I didn't even know what that word meant, so I wrote it down and decided I'd seek more understanding about it in the morning.

The next day, during my prayer time, the Lord began to open up my understanding.

Oxford Dictionary defines *scourging* as:

1. *whip (someone) as a punishment.*

2. *cause great suffering to.*

Though I wasn't being physically whipped, I definitely felt the pain of great suffering!

Immediately upon reading the definition, I was reminded of a dream the Lord gave me.

Sonic Blast

In the dream, I'm negotiating to take the punishment for something my young daughter is being charged with. The punishing rod, so to speak, was a Sonic Cannon—like what was used in *The Incredible Hulk* movie. This acoustic device emits an extremely intense, focused field of compressed sound waves that can disable most assailants.

In the dream, I am unable to fight against the sonic waves, and all I can do is cry out, "Jesus! Jesus!"

In my peripheral vision, I see a preacher being ridiculed and mocked as he's leaving his church.

The dream ends with a very refined woman,

who I believe represents Wisdom, stepping in to block the sonic waves and derailing the punishers so my daughter and I are able to escape.

While reviewing the dream in my journal, I understood that I was being called to stand against the curses attempting to pass down my family line.

As a result, I would suffer intense persecution for His name's sake,[55] but He would send help from Lady Wisdom, who preserves life.[56] He was using my circumstances to teach me how to partner with His Wisdom to shield the attacks.

Take a moment to meditate on the following truths of Scripture (emphasis added):

Hebrews 5:8 NLT

> *8 "Even though <u>Jesus</u> was God's Son, he <u>learned obedience from what he suffered.</u>"*

---

[55] Acts 9:16
[56] Ecclesiastes 7:12

Acts 9:15-16 TPT

15 "The Lord Yahweh answered him, 'Arise and go! I have chosen this man to be my special messenger. He will be brought before kings, before many nations, and before the Jewish people to give them the revelation of who I am. **16** <u>And I will show him how much he is destined to suffer because of his passion for me.</u>'"

Revelation 2:10 TPT

10 "<u>Do not yield to fear in the face of the suffering to come</u>, but be aware of this: the devil is about to have some of you thrown into prison <u>to test your faith</u>. For ten days you will have distress, but remain faithful to the day you die and I will give you the victor's crown of life."

Hebrews 2:10 TPT

10 "For now he towers above all creation, for all things exist through him and for him. And that <u>God made him, pioneer of our salvation, perfect through his sufferings, for this is how he brings many sons and daughters to share in his glory.</u>"

2 Timothy 3: 12-17 TPT

12 "<u>For all who choose to live passionately and faithfully as worshipers of Jesus, the Anointed One, will also experience persecution.</u>

13 "But the evil men and sorcerers will progress from bad to worse, deceived and deceiving, as they lead people further from the truth. **14** Yet you must continue to advance in strength with the truth wrapped around your heart, being assured by God that he's the One who has truly taught you all *these things.*

***15** "Remember what you were taught from your childhood from the Holy Scrolls which can impart to you wisdom to experience everlasting life through the faith of Jesus, the Anointed One! **16** Every Scripture has been written by the Holy Spirit, the breath of God. It will empower you by its instruction and correction, giving you the strength to take the right direction and lead you deeper into the path of godliness. **17** <u>Then you will be God's servant, fully mature and perfectly prepared to fulfill any assignment God gives you</u>."*

Romans 8:17-18 TPT

---

17 "And since we are his true children, we qualify to share all his treasures, for indeed, we are heirs of God himself. And since we are joined to Christ, we also inherit all that he is and all that he has. <u>We will experience being co-glorified with him provided that we</u>

accept his sufferings as our own.

18 *"I am convinced that any suffering we endure is less than nothing compared to the magnitude of glory that is about to be unveiled within us."*

Further Meditation

1. Have you ever experienced persecution for your faith, or been afraid to speak about Jesus?

2. How do you feel about the idea of suffering for God's glory?

Chapter 7: Pitfalls of Pride

Experiencing the power of God can be quite intoxicating, so we really must take caution to use it in alignment with His perfect will.

The Scriptures clearly reveal there are many who use the the Lord's name, merely to serve their own purpose and egos.

The pharisees and sadducees lorded their positions over the people to gain favor and recognition for themselves. Sadly, it happens more frequently than one may think, and is a sign of the end times.

As we explored in *Chapter 3: Honoring Word & Spirit*, the name of Jesus is to be revered with holy awe!

It's a real danger when we place ourselves in the position of being someone else's savior. Unfortunately, I've learned this from personal experience and the Lord has been very stern in His correction.

On many occasions of praying for people, they have thanked *me* for healing them, but I am quick share that it is *Jesus* who has healed them, not me. I don't mind receiving thanks for being faithful in following the Lord's guidance, but the glory of His power belongs to Him alone!

We can accept compliments in a way that does not give glory to our own abilities, but instead points to the wonderful gift of glory He has placed within His children.

By making it clear it is our union with the Lord that releases His power, it serves as an invitation to the prayer recipient to seek the same for themselves.

Deliverance for Dollars

In 2016, I was engaged in an intense season of self-deliverance prayers, while on an extended fast. I felt so empowered, as I could actually feel the demons leaving my body with each passing prayer!

After a particularly triumphant prayer session, I was praising the Lord and exclaiming, "This is so cool! More people need to know about this!"

Suddenly I heard an invisible voice say, "Yeah, and you can make a lot of money with it!"

"Eww!" I exclaimed, "Get out of here devil!"

If Satan can't convince you to give up doing the Lord's work, he'll do everything in his power to pervert it.

Some time after that revelation, I was at a deliverance conference and met a woman I'll call, Macy (not her real name). She had apparently been riddled with demons, and from appearances, it seemed she was radically delivered through the leader's intercession.

During the conference, the Lord gave me a word of knowledge about a cursed piece of jewelry Macy was wearing. After sharing the information with her privately, she asked to exchange contact info. I was a bit reluctant at first, mainly because something just didn't feel right, but decided to ignore the warning out of fear I would cause her to feel rejected. We are all in process!

After the conference, Macy called many times saying she was under attack and needed deliverance, so I would pray for her. Each time she'd end our phone conversations with gushing praises about how powerful my prayers were and that I should be doing this publicly, or as part of a big ministry.

Just as before, I redirected the praises back to Jesus and encouraged her with tips on how to build her own intimacy with Him.

It wasn't long before she was calling me multiple times in a week for deliverance prayers.

I became very annoyed because it seemed Macy blatantly disregarded any wisdom the Lord would share.

Then one day she called and the Lord said, "Tell her she needs to come to *Me* for help."

I relayed the message as the Lord instructed, and prayed for her connection with Him to be strengthened. Right away, she started laying a heavy guilt trip on me saying she's tried, but can't hear the Lord like I do.

Again, I gave her some guidance on ways to connect with Him, but she hurriedly said, "I gotta go!" and hung up the phone.

About a week or so later, she called again, but this time, the Lord sternly warned me, "Do not answer her calls."

Well I thought perhaps that was the enemy trying to trick me, so I asked, "Aren't we called to sacrifice ourselves to help others, Lord?"

The Lord then told me Macy was putting me in the position of being her savior, and the Spirit of Pride was using her to lay a snare for me. *Yikes!!*

So I let her call go to voicemail — and the next one, and the next one, waiting for the Lord to give me the ok to answer, but He never did.

From that point on, Macy's messages escalated from begging me to help her, to calling me vulgar names for not helping.

So often I questioned whether I was hearing the Lord correctly, and each time, He would make it clear to me through a dream or vision, confirming I was not to answer her calls.

In a similar instance, a new friend I had met through a prayer meeting, called and said she was being attacked by a demon through her daughter. She asked if I would come over and pray with her, but the Lord restricted me from doing so, saying, "I am teaching her to call on Me directly with her prayers."

When I shared this with her, she was encouraged and thanked me. Now, she is one of the strongest prayer warriors I know because she embraced the Holy Spirit as her Teacher, instead of relying on me!

It can be very difficult to say no when someone asks for help. But I've learned from these experiences, that guilt and pride often work in tandem to manipulate believers into compromising positions.

Guilt says you have the means to help but aren't doing anything, and Pride says you're the only one who can help. Well, the Lord can drop manna from the sky, or speak through a donkey, when He so chooses![57]

We certainly don't want to interfere with what the Lord is doing in a person's life, so we must get in the habit of asking Him what to do *in each case*, even if you're close friends with the person.

Out of respect for Him, take a moment to pause and wait for His instructions before you pray. You might be surprised by what you hear! Of course, always test the revelation by weighing it against the whole of Scripture.

---

[57] John 6:31; Numbers 22:28

Allow me to share another point of illustration on this. There's a brother in the faith who always introduced me to others as a *"very anointed woman of God."*

At first I was honored by the introduction, because it felt like a marker of intimacy with the Lord. Then after a few times, something just didn't quite feel right about it. I didn't know how to handle the matter, because I didn't sense the brother intended any harm by it.

One day, I asked the Lord what I should say in response, and He happily offered, "Tell them you are *joined* to the Anointed One."

Yes, indeed! That felt much better in my spirit. The next time that brother introduced me, I felt much more peace about my response.

Praying for Profit

Ok, in this next testimony, I'm choosing to be very transparent, in hopes that it will help someone reading this.

I was visiting a friend's church for a special

holiday event, and during fellowship time, the Lord gave me some very specific words of knowledge and prophetic words for several individuals.

Over the next few days, news of those encounters spread quickly throughout the congregation, and I started receiving in home requests for prayer.

I invited my friend to come along, since she knew the people personally, and by the grace of God, we witnessed many incredible healings and answers to prayer!

Often I would arrive, being greeted with baked goods or homemade dishes, and leave with an envelope of cash or a check.

This was all so new for me, and I felt a bit awkward receiving the gifts. At the same time, I was grateful because the gifts helped to offset the financial hardship I had been experiencing.

On one particular occasion, I was invited to pray for a woman, and only after feeling the release from the Lord to go, did I discover she lived quite a distance away.

I was worried about covering the cost of travel which led my thoughts to wonder if she would give an offering as the others had.

Unfortunately, I engaged with the fearful thoughts and made an internal decision to postpone going since she may not give an offering. Oh how I thank God for his mercy and grace!

Like gradually pressing down on the gas pedal, the disapproval of the Lord grew stronger and stronger throughout the day until I was overcome with such sorrow about my selfish decision.

"How could I have been so shallow?" I thought, thinking only of myself and not believing the Lord could take care of my needs. Essentially, I was protecting my own interests and not pursuing what God had instructed me to do.

I quickly repented and asked the Lord to help strengthen my trust in Him. He is so faithful to forgive when we are sincerely sorry, and to cleanse us of the unrighteous fear that hinders us.[58]

I immediately called the woman to make arrangements to visit her.

After ministering with the woman, she handed me a substantial check and said God put it on her heart to give in faith. I checked in with Holy Spirit and heard Him say, "Tis better to give than receive, and I will bless her obedience. Do not reject the gift."

Thank God He is constantly teaching and refining us to become more like Jesus! I'm so grateful for His correction because if I had not gone, I believe it would have given the spirits of pride and greed a foothold in my life.

I believe we all start with some measure of pride, and through our submission to the Holy Spirit and the sanctification process, little by little, that pride is transformed into humility.

Sanctification is a process, so don't beat yourself up *when* you mess up. Remember —

---

[58] 1 John 1:9

though the righteous fall seven times, they shall rise again.[59]

We learn through our mistakes, and must choose to remain teachable in order to embrace God's wisdom.[60] If you've fallen into the trap of pride or greed, take time to repent. God is faithful to forgive and cleanse us.[61]

Consider the implications of the following passages of Scripture (emphasis added):

Philippians 2:21 ESV

21 "For they all <u>seek their own interests</u>, not those of Jesus Christ."

---

1 Peter 5:2 NLT

2 "Care for the flock that God has entrusted to you. Watch over it willingly, not

---

[59] Proverbs 24:16
[60] Proverbs 12:1, 19:20; 13:18
[61] 1 John 1:9

> *grudgingly—<u>not for what you will get out of it</u>, but because you are eager to serve God."*

Titus 1:7

> *7 "For an overseer, as God's steward, must be above reproach. <u>He must not be arrogant</u> or quick-tempered or a drunkard or violent or <u>greedy for gain,</u>"*

1 Timothy 3:8 TPT

> *8 "And in the same way the deacons must be those who are pure and true to their word, <u>not addicted to wine, or with greedy eyes on the contributions.</u>"*

Let's aim to be humble heroes like Jesus and the great Saints who have gone before us, serving others above ourselves, as the Lord leads.

Jesus never intentionally drew attention to

Himself, or used His position of great power to gain wealth, status, or control over anyone else. He genuinely desired to connect people with the Kingdom of God.

As you venture out to minister in your sphere of influence, be aware, because God's anointing draws attention. However, not all attention is good.

We must pray for the Lord to calibrate our spiritual discernment to help us navigate around the pitfalls of pride—some of which include *idolatry, greed, and jealous envy.* Let's take a look at each one.

Idolatry. According to Webster's Dictionary, idolatry is defined as *"the worship of idols or excessive devotion to, or reverence for, some person or thing."*

Some people will be in awe and want to be around you because of God's powerful presence. To some degree, this can be healthy, as long as the focus remains on helping them develop an ongoing, personal connection with the Lord.

When the people of Lystra witnessed Paul and Barnabas releasing God's power, they began worshipping them as gods. The apostles were mortified and pleaded with the people to stop, identifying themselves as weak humans.[62]

Consider how Paul reveals he was given a messenger of Satan to harass him, in order to keep him from becoming too proud by all the wonderful revelation he received from the Lord.[63]

Remember the Gorilla Gift dream shared back in Chapter 6? The harassing gorilla is identified as a "gift" to keep me humble while in the service of the King!

Seeing God with this understanding may be difficult for some to swallow, but know it originates out of His great plan to mold our character into the likeness of Jesus Christ.

Greed. Oxford defines greed as *"intense and selfish desire for something, especially wealth, power,*

---

[62] Acts 14:11-18
[63] 2 Corinthians 12:7

or food."

Just like the religious leaders of Jesus' day, many people leverage the power of God for money, power, and/or status, either directly, or through the manipulation of God's anointed.

The devil first tempted me with greed when he suggested I could make a lot of money off of people who needed deliverance. At that particular time, I was in a very weak financial position and could have easily fallen prey to the temptation. But greater is He who is in me![64]

Greed can be a subtle trap.

I once wrote in for a prophetic word from a nationally recognized prophet of God. Several months later, I received a response, which was quite accurate.

At the end of his message, however, he instructed me to sow an offering seed "in order for the full anointing of the prophetic word to be released over my life."

---

[64] 1 John 4:4

Immediately, I heard the Holy Spirit say the man was partnering with greed. Though the prophetic word was accurate, the prophet was attempting to sell the anointing.

The Apostle Peter rebuked Simon the Sorcerer for trying to purchase the anointing, saying his heart was not right before God and he was held captive to sin.[65]

Remember, you cannot serve both God and money.[66] It's not that money in itself is bad, but the love of it is the root of all evil.[67]

Jealous Envy. Webster states, *"While many people believe that jealous means fearing someone will take what you have, and envious means desiring what someone else has, historical usage shows that both mean 'covetous' and are interchangeable when describing desiring someone else's possessions.'"*

When Simon offered Peter and John money for God's power, Peter rebuke Simon with, *"I*

---

[65] Acts 8:20-23
[66] Matthew 6:24
[67] 1 Timothy 6:10

discern that jealous envy has poisoned you…"[68]

The Word reveals the religious leaders handed Jesus over to Pilate out of jealous envy.[69] They were so wrapped up in pride, and threatened by the crowds Jesus drew through the miracles He performed. They were constantly challenging Jesus and trying to trap Him in His words.[70]

As you begin to grow in the gifts of the Spirit, there may be others, even well-meaning Christians, who become jealous of how God is working through you, which promotes their own feelings of inadequacy.

Remain humble, and do not boast about the great revelations He is sharing with you, or it may come back to bite you like it did with Joseph and his jealous brothers.

Televangelist Trap

To further illustrate my understanding of how

---

[68] Acts 8:23 TPT
[69] Matthew 27:18
[70] Matthew 22:15-22

these pitfalls often overlap, I'll share a personal experience.

I was invited to attend a special event hosted by a famous televangelist. At first, I was reluctant to go because I had received several dreams about this person posing as a Christian, which I found peculiar because I had not listened to his messages. When I asked the Lord about the event, I felt released to "go with caution."

Before entering the arena, I pleaded the blood of Jesus over my mind, and asked the Lord to calibrate my senses to the leading of Holy Spirit.

Shortly after the event was underway, I began experiencing an unusual drowsiness and agitation in my eyes, causing them to water excessively. When I inquired of the Lord, I was quite surprised to hear Him say, "The people are being hypnotized."

Immediately feeling revived by the Lord's word, I quickly searched Google and found Oxford's definition of hypnosis as "the induction of a state of consciousness in which a person

<u>loses the power of voluntary action and is highly responsive to suggestion or direction</u>" (emphasis added).

Wow! This dangerously imposes on a person's free will to choose and opens them up to demonic influence!

Interestingly, as I've been writing about this experience, I felt prompted to research a little further, and am amazed to discover *drowsiness* and *watery eyes* are among the signs of hypnosis.[71] The Holy Spirit cued the gift of spiritual discernment through my physical senses!

I also understood, the underlying motive of the event was to promote the televangelist's "brand" in order to sell books. So even though this man spoke about Jesus, he was doing so, not out of love for Him, but for personal gain.

Jesus warns of many who will do great things in His name, but will not enter the Kingdom of

---

[71] Elman, D. (1984). *Hypnotherapy*. Glendale, California: Westwood Publishing. (Original work published as Findings in Hypnosis, 1964).

Heaven, because they do so apart from Him.[72]

After the "show," the person who invited me arranged for us to meet the televangelist. Before approaching him with outstretched hand, I silently pleaded the blood of Jesus over my mind and asked the Lord what He wanted to show me.

When I shook the man's hand, I received a vision of a smaller version of himself being trapped inside his own body, and understood this to mean he was extremely insecure and driven by the opinions of others. The fame served to validate his self-worth.

Furthermore, the Lord revealed this world famous man was under the influence of controlling spirits—some of whom were operating through his own family members, as they used his position to advance their own agendas.

We have a biblical picture of this same type of pitfall with King Saul, who feared others above

---

[72] Matthew 7:21-22

God.[73] His repeated acts of rebellion against the Lord caused the removal of God's Holy Spirit from Saul, and saddled him with a tormenting spirit.[74]

I too had nearly been taken captive by pride's deception when I initially disobeyed God's instructions to go and pray for that woman who lived far away from me.

My motives were tainted the moment I relegated ministry as a means for gaining provisions, instead of focusing on spreading His Kingdom and Righteousness.

I thank God for alerting me to that trap and cleansing me of those unrighteous thoughts!

It is a great responsibility to carry the Lord's power, and we need His ongoing help to steward it for His purposes.

The supernatural gifts and insights from the Holy Spirit are meant to equip the saints for

---

[73] 1 Samuel 15:24
[74] 1 Samual 16:14

ministry and to build up the body of believers,[75] not for our own popularity and comfort.

After parting ways with the televangelist, I felt a deep sadness for him and prayed for his union with Christ to be strengthened.

As you go forth, be mindful to remain humble under the mighty hand of the Lord, so you will be delivered from every hidden trap of the enemy.

Here are a few Scriptures to meditate upon as you move forward in the King's service (emphasis added):

1 John 2:15-17 TPT

15 "Don't set the affections of your heart on this world or in loving the things of the world. The love of the Father and the love of the world are incompatible. 16 <u>For all that the world can offer us—the gratification of our flesh, the allurement of the things of the</u>

---

[75] Ephesians 4:12

world, and the obsession with status and importance—none of these things come from the Father but from the world. 17 This world and its desires are in the process of passing away, but those who love to do the will of God live forever."

Proverbs 22:4 AMP

4 "*The reward of humility* [that is, having a realistic view of one's importance] *and the* [reverent, worshipful] *fear of the Lord*
Is riches, honor, and life."

Psalm 149:4 TPT

4 "For he enjoys his faithful lovers.
He adorns the humble with his beauty
and he loves to give them the victory."

1 Peter 5:6-7 AMP

6 "Therefore <u>humble yourselves under the mighty hand of God [set aside self-righteous pride], so that He may exalt you [to a place of honor in His service] at the appropriate time,</u> **7** casting all your cares [all your anxieties, all your worries, and all your concerns, once and for all] on Him, for He cares about you [with deepest affection, and watches over you very carefully]."

Philippians 2:3-9 TPT

3 "<u>Be free from pride-filled opinions, for they will only harm your cherished unity.</u> Don't allow self-promotion to hide in your hearts, but in authentic humility put others first and view others as more important than yourselves. **4** Abandon every display of selfishness. Possess a greater concern for what matters to others instead of your own interests. **5** And consider the example that

Jesus, the Anointed One, has set before us. Let his mindset become your motivation.

6 "*He existed in the form of God, yet he gave no thought to seizing equality with God as his supreme prize.*[d] **7** Instead he emptied himself of his outward glory by reducing himself to the form of a lowly servant. He became human! **8** He humbled himself and became vulnerable, choosing to be revealed as a man and was obedient. He was a perfect example, even in his death—a criminal's death by crucifixion!

9 "Because of that obedience, God exalted him and multiplied his greatness! He has now been given the greatest of all names!"

Footnote [d]: Philippians 2:6, Or "*as something to be exploited.*"

Luke 14:10-11 MSG

__10-11__ "When you're invited to dinner, go and sit at the last place. Then when the host comes he may very well say, 'Friend, come up to the front.' That will give the dinner guests something to talk about! What I'm saying is, If you <u>walk around with your nose in the air, you're going to end up flat on your face. But if you're content to be simply yourself, you will become more than yourself.</u>"

Further Meditation

1. Have you ever fallen into the trap of pride?

2. If you're in ministry, ask Holy Spirit to reveal if there is any part of you trying to gain something for yourself, or trying to prove your worth to others?

Commission

Now go forth in the power of God's Spirit to release His Kingdom and Righteousness!

Remain humble and aware that it is our Heavenly Father who has chosen you to carry His glory.

Steward it well, and in accordance with His unique plan for your life.

May God bless you with grace and favor!

ABOUT THE AUTHOR

Author. Angela writes about her experiences as a prophetic minister, teaching others how to draw closer to the person of Jesus Christ, partner with the Holy Spirit, and come into alignment with our Heavenly Father's divine plans.

Advocate. As a survivor and overcomer of domestic and sexual violence, Angela is passionate about helping others return to wholeness. After completing 80 hours of victim advocacy training through *A Safe Place* and *Zacharias Center,* Angela began volunteering her time to serve *Stepping Stones Network*—an organization devoted to providing restorative care services to survivors of domestic commercial sexual exploitation.

Advisor. Angela holds a BA degree in Marketing from Middle TN State University, and carries more than two decades of experience in corporate and national sales markets. She currently serves as a freelance advisor to business and ministry leaders.

Artist. Angela is often found releasing creative expressions through singing, songwriting, poetry, painting, sketching, photography, and fashion design projects. She is also currently learning to play the piano, together with her daughter.

Angela's greatest blessing is the gift of motherhood to her three beautiful children—Luke, Brody, and Zarrah. Along with their pets, Bella the yorkie, and Daisy the guinea pig, Angela dreams of living on a horse farm, where others can come to receive healing and refreshment.

For more information, please visit:

www.AngelaAttiah.com

OTHER BOOKS

Rescue Mission: Prisoners of Darkness

A true story of healing and reconciliation for those who long to break free from the bondage of sexual and domestic violence.

Available on Amazon!

UPCOMING RELEASES...

The Victor's Crown of Life: Dying to Self and Living For Christ

A personal account of triumphant faith, revealing how God uses trials and suffering to release a greater measure of His glory.

The Era of Immortality: Breaking And Reversing the Curse of Aging!

The unveiling of God's appointed time for His Bride to rule and reign over death, the last enemy to be destroyed!

www.ingramcontent.com/pod-product-compliance
Lightning Source LLC
Chambersburg PA
CBHW070200100426
42743CB00013B/2993